A PULPIT MANUAL

A PULPIT MANUAL

Prepared by
DONALD E. DEMARAY

BAKER BOOK HOUSE
Grand Rapids   Michigan

Library of Congress Catalog Card Number: 59-15526

Copyright, 1959, by
BAKER BOOK HOUSE

ISBN: 0-8010-2815-9

PHOTOLITHOPRINTED BY CUSHING - MALLOY, INC.
ANN ARBOR, MICHIGAN, UNITED STATES OF AMERICA
1 9 7 1

To

Donald and Lydia McNichols
who know the meaning of worship
in its finest tradition

PREFACE

This is a ready-reference manual. It is designed to be taken right into the pulpit for use in the service of worship. *A Pulpit Manual* was prompted by the very real need of the busy pastor to lay his hands on worship materials quickly and easily.

All materials in this volume have been taken either from the Bible or from the acknowledged leaders of the Church (Augustine, Luther, Wesley, etc.). It is believed that this basis of selection will help make for worship services of a more Biblical and historical character.

This project was suggested to me by my father, C. Dorr Demaray. Without his persistent suggestion that a manual of this type be done, I would never have undertaken the making of this book.

DONALD E. DEMARAY

School of Religion
Seattle Pacific College

CONTENTS

I. CALLS TO WORSHIP

CALLS TO WORSHIP

...The hour cometh, and now is, when the true worshippers shall worship the Father in spirit and in truth: for the Father seeketh such to worship him. God *is* a Spirit: and they that worship him must worship *him* in spirit and in truth.

JOHN 4:23-24

Make a joyful noise unto the Lord, all ye lands. Serve the Lord with gladness: come before his presence with singing.

PSALM 100:1-2

Enter into his gates with thanksgiving, and into his courts with praise: be thankful unto him, and bless his name. For the Lord is good; his mercy is everlasting; and his truth endureth to all generations.

PSALM 100:4-5

Let us come before his presence with thanksgiving, and make a joyful noise unto him with psalms.

PSALM 95:2

One thing have I desired of the Lord, that will I seek after; that I may dwell in the house of the Lord all the days of my life, to behold the beauty of the Lord, and to enquire in his temple. For in the time of trouble he shall hide me in his pavilion: in the secret of his tabernacle shall be hide me; he shall set me up upon a rock.

PSALM 27:4-5

As the hart panteth after the water brooks, so panteth my soul after thee, O God. My soul thirsteth for God, for the living God: when shall I come and appear before God?

PSALM 42:1-2

O come, let us worship and bow down: let us kneel before the Lord our maker.

PSALM 95:6

He that dwelleth in the secret place of the Most High shall abide under the shadow of the Almighty.   PSALM 91:1

Give unto the Lord the glory due unto his name; worship the Lord in the beauty of holiness.   PSALM 29:2

...The Lord is my rock, and my fortress, and my deliverer; The God of my rock; in him will I trust; he is my shield, and the horn of my salvation, my high tower, and my refuge, my saviour; thou savest me from violence. I will call on the Lord, who is worthy to be praised: so shall I be saved from mine enemies.   II SAMUEL 22:2-4

...I saw also the Lord sitting upon a throne, high and lifted up, and his train filled the temple .... Holy, holy, holy, is the Lord of hosts: the whole earth is full of his glory.

ISAIAH 6:1, 3

. . . The Lord, whom ye seek, shall suddenly come to his temple, even the messenger of the covenant, whom ye delight in: behold, he shall come, saith the Lord of hosts.

MALACHI 3:1

Be still, and know that I am God: I will be exalted among the heathen, I will be exalted in the earth. The Lord of hosts is with us; the God of Jacob is our refuge.   PSALM 46:10-11

O send out thy light and thy truth: let them lead me; let them bring me unto thy holy hill, and to thy tabernacles.

PSALM 43:3

The Lord is nigh unto them that are of a broken heart; and saveth such as be of a contrite spirit.   PSALM 34:18

Seek ye the Lord while he may be found, call ye upon him while he is near.   ISAIAH 55:6

Surely the righteous shall give thanks unto thy name: the upright shall dwell in thy presence. PSALM 140:13

Exalt ye the Lord our God, and worship at his footstool; for he is holy. . . .Exalt the Lord our God, and worship at his holy hill; for the Lord our God is holy. PSALM 99:5, 9

I will worship toward thy holy temple, and praise thy name for thy lovingkindness and for thy truth: for thou hast magnified thy word above all thy name. PSALM 138:2

Lift up your hands in the sanctuary, and bless the Lord.
PSALM 134:2

Calls to Worship for Holy Days

THE NEW YEAR

...I have set before thee an open door, and no man can shut it.... REVELATION 3:8

PALM SUNDAY

Rejoice greatly, O daughter of Zion; shout, O daughter of Jerusalem: behold, thy King cometh unto thee: he is just, and having salvation; lowly, and riding upon an ass, and upon a colt the foal of an ass. ZECHARIAH 9:9

GOOD FRIDAY

Is it nothing to you, all ye that pass by? behold, and see if there be any sorrow like unto my sorrow, which is done unto me.... LAMENTATIONS 1:12

EASTER

...Fear not; I am the first and the last: I am he that liveth, and was dead; and, behold, I am alive for evermore, Amen.... REVELATION 1:17-18

CHRISTMAS

For unto us a child is born, unto us a son is given: and the government shall be upon his shoulder: and his name shall be called Wonderful, Counsellor, The mighty God, The everlasting Father, The Prince of Peace. ISAIAH 9:6

ASCENSION SUNDAY

Ye men of Galilee, why stand ye gazing up into heaven? this same Jesus, which is taken up from you into heaven, shall so come in like manner as ye have seen him go into heaven. ACTS 1:11

But ye shall receive power, after that the Holy Spirit is come upon you: and ye shall be witnesses unto me both in Jerusalem, and in all Judaea, and in Samaria, and unto the uttermost part of the earth. ACTS 1:8

Calls to Worship for Special Sundays

RACE RELATIONS SUNDAY (BROTHERHOOD DAY)

All the ends of the world shall remember and turn unto the Lord: and all the kindreds of the nations shall worship before thee.   PSALM 22:27

STEWARDSHIP SUNDAY (TITHING SUNDAY)

But seek ye first the kingdom of God, and his righteousness; and all these things shall be added unto you.

MATTHEW 6:33

CHRISTIAN EDUCATION SUNDAY

Take my yoke upon you, and learn of me; for I am meek and lowly in heart: and ye shall find rest unto your souls.

MATTHEW 11:29

MOTHER'S DAY (FAMILY SUNDAY)

And Ruth said, Intreat me not to leave thee, or to return from following after thee: for whither thou goest, I will go; and where thou lodgest, I will lodge: thy people shall be my people, and thy God my God.   RUTH 1:16

MEMORIAL SUNDAY

...God is our God for ever and ever: he will be our guide even unto death.   PSALM 48:14

LABOR DAY SUNDAY

Six days shalt thou labor, and do all thy work: But the seventh day is the sabbath of the Lord thy God....

EXODUS 20:9-10

INDEPENDENCE SUNDAY

Blessed is the nation whose God is the Lord; and the people whom he hath chosen for his own inheritance.... Let thy mercy, O Lord, be upon us, according as we hope in thee.

PSALM 33:12, 22

WORLD WIDE COMMUNION SUNDAY

. . . The bread of God is he which cometh down from heaven, and giveth life unto the world.   JOHN 6:33

MEN AND MISSIONS SUNDAY

Go ye therefore, and teach all nations, baptizing them in the name of the Father, and of the Son, and of the Holy Spirit.   MATTHEW 28:19

REFORMATION SUNDAY

For I am not ashamed of the gospel of Christ; for it is the power of God unto salvation to every one that believeth; to the Jew first, and also to the Greek. For therein is the righteousness of God revealed from faith to faith: as it is written, The just shall live by faith.   ROMANS 1:16-17

WORLD PEACE SUNDAY (WORLD ORDER SUNDAY)

And many nations shall come, and say, Come, and let us go up to the mountain of the Lord, and to the house of the God of Jacob; and he will teach us of his ways, and we will walk in his paths: for the law shall go forth of Zion, and the word of the Lord from Jerusalem.   MICAH 4:2

THANKSGIVING SUNDAY

. . . Blessing, and glory, and wisdom, and thanksgiving, and honour, and power, and might, be unto our God for ever and ever. Amen.   REVELATION 7:12

UNIVERSAL BIBLE SUNDAY

Thy word is a lamp unto my feet, and a light unto my path.   PSALM 119:105

LAYMEN'S DAY

Watch ye, stand fast in the faith, quit you like men, be strong.   I CORINTHIANS 16:13

II. INVOCATIONS AND OPENING PRAYERS

INVOCATIONS AND OPENING PRAYERS

May God, who seeth all things, and who is the Ruler of all spirits and the Lord of all flesh — who chose our Lord Jesus Christ and us through Him to be a peculiar people — grant to every soul that calleth upon His glorious and holy Name, faith, peace, patience, long-suffering, self-control, purity, and sobriety, to the well-pleasing of His Name, through our High Priest and Protector, Jesus Christ, by whom be to Him glory, and majesty, and power, and honour, both now and forevermore. Amen. CLEMENT OF ROME

Merciful Lord, the Comforter and Teacher of Thy faithful people, increase in Thy Church the desires which Thou hast given, and confirm the hearts of those who hope in Thee by enabling them to understand the depth of Thy promises, that all Thine adopted sons may even now behold, with the eyes of faith, and patiently wait for, the light which as yet Thou dost not openly manifest; through Jesus Christ our Lord. Amen. AMBROSE OF MILAN

O God, Who didst look on man when he had fallen down into death, and resolve to redeem him by the advent of Thine only begotten Son; grant, we beseech Thee, that they who confess His glorious Incarnation may also be admitted to the fellowship of Him their Redeemer, through the same Jesus Christ our Lord. Amen. AMBROSE OF MILAN

Almighty God, who hast given us grace at this time to make our common supplications unto Thee; and dost promise that when two or three are gathered together in Thy name Thou wilt grant their requests: fulfill now, O Lord, the desires and petitions of Thy servants, as may be most expedient for them, granting us in this world knowledge of Thy truth, and in the world to come, life everlasting. Amen. CHRYSOSTOM

O God, the light of every heart that sees Thee, the Life of every soul that loves Thee, the strength of every mind that seeks Thee, grant me ever to continue steadfast in Thy holy love. Be Thou the joy of my heart; take it all to Thyself, and therein abide. The house of my soul is, I confess, too narrow for Thee; do thou enlarge it, that Thou mayest enter in.... Amen.   ST. AUGUSTINE

Let our souls ever seek Thee, and let us persist in seeking, till we have found, and are in full possession of Thee. Amen.
                                              ST. AUGUSTINE (adapted)

Thou bounteous Giver of all good gifts, give to him who is weary refreshing food; gather our distracted thoughts and powers into harmony again; and set the prisoner free. See, he stands at thy door and knocks; be it open to him, that he may enter with a free step, and be quickened by Thee. For Thou art the Well-spring of Life, the Light of eternal Brightness . . . . Amen.   ST. AUGUSTINE

O glorious King, Lord of all power, who triumphing this day didst ascend above the heavens, leave us not orphans, but send down on us, from the Father, the spirit of truth which Thou hast promised. Amen.   BEDE THE VENERABLE

Lord, make me an instrument of Thy peace. Where there is hatred, let me sow love; where there is injury, pardon; where there is doubt, faith; where there is despair, hope; where there is darkness, light; where sadness, joy.

O Divine Master, grant that I may not so much seek to be consoled as to console; to be understood as to understand; to be loved as to love; for it is in giving that we receive; it is in pardoning that we are pardoned; and it is in dying that we are born to eternal love. Amen.   FRANCIS OF ASSISI

24

Great art Thou, O Lord, and greatly to be praised; great is Thy power, and Thy wisdom is infinite. Thee would we praise without ceasing. Thou callest us to delight in Thy praise, for Thou hast made us for Thyself, and our hearts find no rest until we rest in Thee; Who with the Father and the Holy Ghost all glory, praise, and honour be ascribed, both now and forevermore. Amen.   ST. AUGUSTINE

Strengthen us, O God, by the grace of Thy Holy Spirit. Grant us to be strengthened with might in the inner man, and to empty our hearts of all useless care and anguish. O Lord, grant us heavenly wisdom, that we may learn above all things to seek and to find Thee, above all things to . . . love Thee, and to think of all other things as being, what indeed they are, at the disposal of Thy wisdom. Amen.
THOMAS A KEMPIS (adapted)

O Thou who art the everlasting Essence of things beyond space and time and yet within them; Thou who transcendest yet pervadest all things, manifest Thyself unto us, feeling after Thee, seeking Thee in the shades of ignorance. Stretch forth Thy hand to help us, who cannot without Thee come to Thee; and reveal Thyself unto us, who seek nothing beside Thee; through Jesus Christ our Lord. Amen.
JOHN SCOTUS (Erigena)

Grant us, even us, O Lord, to know Thee, and love Thee, and rejoice in Thee. And if we cannot do these perfectly in this life, let us, at least, advance to higher degrees every day, till we can come to do them in perfection. Let our knowledge, love, and joy of Thee increase in us here, that they may be full hereafter. . . . O make good Thy gracious promises to us, that our joy may be full. To Thine honour and glory, Who with the Father and the Holy Ghost liveth and reigneth one God, world without end. Amen.   ST. AUGUSTINE (adapted)

Look upon us, O Lord, and let all the darkness of our souls vanish before the beams of Thy brightness. Fill us with holy love, and open to us the treasures of Thy wisdom. Amen.

St. Augustine

Oh come, Thou refreshment of them that languish and faint. Come, Thou Star and Guide of them that sail in the tempestuous sea of the world; Thou only Haven of the tossed and ship-wrecked. Come, Thou Glory and Crown of the living, and only Safeguard of the dying. Come, Holy Spirit, in much mercy, and make me fit to receive Thee. Amen.

St. Augustine

O God our Father, who dost exhort us to pray and worship thee; hear us who are trembling in darkness, and stretch forth Thy hand unto us; hold forth Thy light before us; recall us from our wanderings; and, Thou being our Guide, may we be restored to our true selves and to Thee, through Jesus Christ. Amen.

St. Augustine (adapted)

We humble ourselves, O Lord of heaven and earth, before thy glorious majesty. We acknowledge thy eternal power, wisdom, goodness and truth, and desire to render unto thee thanks for all the benefits which thou pourest upon us. But, above all, for thine inestimable love in the redemption of us by our Lord Jesus Christ. Amen.

John Wesley

Be, Lord, within to strengthen us, without to guard us, over to shelter us, beneath to stablish us, before to guide us, after to forward us, round about to secure us. Amen.

Lancelot Andrewes (adapted)

Almighty God, grant us the forgiveness of all our sins that we, being full of grace, virtue and good works, may become thy kingdom. May we with heart, soul, mind and strength, inwardly and outwardly, submit to thy commands and do thy will. Amen.

Martin Luther

O Lord our God, grant us grace to desire Thee with our whole heart, that so desiring, we may seek and find Thee; and so finding Thee we may love Thee; and loving Thee we may hate those sins from which Thou hast redeemed us; for the sake of Jesus Christ. Amen.   St. Anselm

Invocations and Opening Prayers for Holy Days

THE NEW YEAR

O Thou Who art ever the same, grant us so to pass through the coming year with faithful hearts, that we may be able in all things to please Thy loving eyes; through Jesus Christ our Lord. Amen.　　MOZARABIC LITURGY (before A.D. 700)

PALM SUNDAY

... Blessed is he that cometh in the name of the Lord: Blessed be the kingdom of our father David, that cometh in the name of the Lord: Hosanna in the highest. Amen.　　MARK 11:9-10

GOOD FRIDAY

We implore Thee, by the memory of Thy Cross's hallowed and most bitter anguish, make us fear Thee, make us love Thee, O Christ. Amen.　　ST. BRIDGET OF IRELAND

EASTER

O Lord Jesus Christ, by Thy glorious resurrection, in which Thou didst appear alive and immortal to Thy disciples and faithful followers, by Thy forty days' abiding and sweet converse, in which by many infallible proofs, speaking of things pertaining to the Kingdom of God, Thou didst comfort them and assure them of Thine actual resurrection, removing all doubt from their hearts. We beseech Thee, O Lord, grant that we may be numbered among those who were foreordained by God to be witnesses of Thy resurrection, not only by word of mouth, but in reality of good works; for Thine honour and glory, who with the Father and the Holy Ghost livest and reignest ever one God, world without end. Amen.

LUDOLF OF SAXONY

28

ASCENSION SUNDAY

Grant, we beseech thee, almighty God, that like as we do believe thy only-begotten Son, our Lord Jesus Christ, to have ascended into the heavens; so may we also in heart and mind thither ascend, and with him continually dwell, who liveth and reigneth with thee and the Holy Spirit, ever one God, world without end. Amen.   MARTIN LUTHER

PENTECOST SUNDAY (WHITSUNDAY)

We beseech Thee, Lord, open Thy heavens; from thence may Thy gifts descend to us. Put forth Thine own hand from heaven and touch our heads. May we feel the touch of Thy hand, and receive the joy of the Holy Spirit, that we may remain blessed for evermore. Amen.

ETHELWOLD OF YORK (adapted)

CHRISTMAS

Now, O Lord, in recollection we shall worship the mysteries of Thy Son and await His birth within our hearts. Come, Lord Jesus, Spirit of Truth and Love .... We await Thee, Lord Jesus, as the prophets and patriarchs of old awaited Thee. Joyfully we repeat with them, 'O heavens, shed thy light, and let thy showers descend upon the just; let the earth be opened that our Saviour may come forth.' ... Amen.

FRANÇOIS FÉNELON (adapted)

Invocations and Opening Prayers for Special Sundays

RACE RELATIONS SUNDAY (BROTHERHOOD DAY)
Pour upon us, O Lord, the spirit of brotherly kindness and peace; so that, sprinkled with the dew of Thy benediction, we may be made glad by Thy glory and grace; through Jesus Christ our Lord. Amen. SARUM BREVIARY

STEWARDSHIP SUNDAY (TITHING SUNDAY)
Almighty God, whose loving hand hath given us all that we possess; Grant us grace that we may honour thee with our substance, and remembering the account which we must one day give, may be faithful stewards of thy bounty; through Jesus Christ our Lord. Amen. THE BOOK OF COMMON PRAYER

CHRISTIAN EDUCATION SUNDAY
And now, we beseech Thee Lord Jesus, that to whom Thou dost vouchsafe sweet draughts of the words of Thy knowledge, Thou wilt also, of Thy goodness, grant that we may, in due time, come to Thee, the fountain of all wisdom, and ever stand before Thy face; for Thy sake. Amen. BEDE THE VENERABLE

MOTHER'S DAY (FAMILY SUNDAY)
Almighty, everlasting God, have mercy on Thy servants our mothers. Keep them continually under Thy protection, and direct them according to Thy gracious favour in the way of everlasting salvation....And forasmuch as they trust in Thy mercy, vouchsafe, O Lord, graciously to assist them with Thy heavenly help, that they may ever diligently serve Thee, and by no temptation be separated from Thee; through Jesus Christ our Lord. Amen. THOMAS À KÉMPIS (adapted)

MEMORIAL SUNDAY
O Lord God, whose blessed Son, our Saviour, gave his back to the smiters and hid not his face from shame; Grant us grace to take joyfully the sufferings of the present time, in full assur-

ance of the glory that shall be revealed; through the same thy
Son Jesus Christ our Lord. Amen.

THE BOOK OF COMMON PRAYER

LABOR DAY SUNDAY

Teach us, good Lord, to serve thee as thou deservest; to give
and not to count the cost; to fight and not to heed the wounds;
to toil and not to seek for rest; to labor and not to ask for any
reward, save that of knowing that we do thy will; through
Jesus Christ, our Lord. Amen.

IGNATIUS LOYOLA

INDEPENDENCE SUNDAY

O Eternal God, through whose mighty power our fathers
won their liberties of old; Grant, we beseech thee, that we and
all the people of this land may have grace to maintain these
liberties in righteousness and peace; through Jesus Christ our
Lord. Amen.

THE BOOK OF COMMON PRAYER

WORLD WIDE COMMUNION SUNDAY

Thou art blessed, O Lord, who nourishest our spirits, who
givest us the food of holy bread and drink. Fill the hearts of
thy children around the world, this day, with joy and gladness,
that having always what is sufficient for them, they may
abound to every good work, in Christ Jesus our Lord, through
whom glory, honour, and power be to Thee forever. Amen.

APOSTOLIC CONSTITUTIONS (adapted)

MEN AND MISSIONS SUNDAY

Remember, O Lord, all who in heathen lands are under instruction for Holy Baptism; have mercy upon them and confirm them in the faith; remove all the remains of idolatry and
superstition from their hearts, that being devoted to Thy
law, Thy precepts, Thy fear, Thy truths, and Thy commandments, they may grow to a firm knowledge of the word in
which they have been instructed, and may be found worthy
to be made an inhabitation of the Holy Ghost, by the laver
of regeneration, for the remission of their sins; through Jesus
Christ our Lord. Amen.

ST. BASIL

REFORMATION SUNDAY

Almighty God, grant that all preachers may proclaim Christ and thy word with power and blessing everywhere. Grant that all who hear thy word preached may learn to know Christ and amend their ways. Wilt thou also graciously remove from the Church all preaching and teaching which does not honor Christ. Amen.   MARTIN LUTHER

WORLD PEACE SUNDAY (WORLD ORDER SUNDAY)

O God who art Peace everlasting, whose chosen reward is the gift of peace, and who hast taught us that the peacemakers are Thy children, pour Thy peace into our souls, that everything discordant may utterly vanish, and all that makes for peace be sweet to us for ever; through Jesus Christ our Lord. Amen.

MOZARABIC LITURGY

THANKSGIVING SUNDAY

Thanks be to Thee, O Lord Jesus Christ, for food, shelter, and for all material and spiritual blessings which Thou hast given us . . . . O most merciful Redeemer, friend and brother, may we know Thee more clearly, love Thee more dearly, and follow Thee more nearly; for Thine own sake. Amen.

RICHARD OF CHICHESTER (adapted)

UNIVERSAL BIBLE SUNDAY

O Lord, heavenly Father, in whom is the fullness of light and wisdom: Enlighten our minds by thy Holy Spirit and give us grace to receive thy Word with reverence and humility, without which no man can understand thy truth. For Jesus Christ's sake. Amen.   JOHN CALVIN

LAYMEN'S DAY

O fountain of love, love Thou our friends and teach them to love Thee with all their hearts, that they may think and speak and do only such things as are well-pleasing to Thee; through Jesus Christ our Lord. Amen.   ANSELM

III. OFFERTORY SENTENCES AND PRAYERS

OFFERTORY SENTENCES AND PRAYERS

Sentence: Jacob promised God that, "all that thou shalt give me I will surely give the tenth unto thee."

GENESIS 28:22

Prayer: O Lord, our Saviour, who hast warned us that thou wilt require much of those to whom much is given; grant that we whose lot is cast in so goodly a heritage may strive together the more abundantly to extend to others what we so richly enjoy.... Amen.   ST. AUGUSTINE

Sentence: For God so loved the world, that he gave his only begotten Son, that whosoever believeth in him should not perish, but have everlasting life.   JOHN 3:16

Prayer: We give thanks to thee, Lord God Almighty, that thou hast revived us through thy heavenly gift. We pray that by thy mercy we may attain to a firm faith in thee and a fervent love for one another, demonstrated by the very giving of ourselves, through Jesus Christ thy Son our Lord. Amen.

MARTIN LUTHER (adapted)

Sentence: Lay not up for yourselves treasures upon earth, where moth and rust doth corrupt, and where thieves break through and steal: But lay up for yourselves treasures in heaven, where neither moth nor rust doth corrupt, and where thieves do not break through nor steal: For where your treasure is, there will your heart be also.   MATTHEW 6:19-21

Prayer: Teach us, O God, to use this world without abusing it; and to receive the things needful for the body without losing our part in thy love; and put it into our hearts to give wholeheartedly to the cause of Kingdom building. Amen.

JOHN WESLEY (adapted)

Sentence: A good man out of the good treasure of the heart bringeth forth good things.... MATTHEW 12:35

Prayer: Dear God! Let us know Thy great grace and goodness, loving Thee in return, offering ourselves in love unto Thee so that no carnal love may separate us from Thee. Amen. JOHANN ARNDT (adapted)

Sentence: Give unto the Lord the glory due unto his name: bring an offering, and come before him: worship the Lord in the beauty of holiness. I CHRONICLES 16:29

Prayer: Our Father God, we doubt not that the things for which we plead will be granted, not because we have requested them but because thou hast commanded us to pray for them and hast certainly promised them. Amen.

MARTIN LUTHER (adapted)

Sentence: ... The children of Israel bring an offering in a clean vessel into the house of the Lord. ISAIAH 66:20

Prayer: Direct us, O Lord, in all our doings, with thy most gracious favour, and further us with thy continual help; that in all our works begun, continued, and ended in thee, we may glorify thy holy Name, and finally, by thy mercy, obtain everlasting life; through Jesus Christ our Lord. Amen.

THE BOOK OF COMMON PRAYER

Sentence: Give unto the Lord the glory due unto his name: bring an offering, and come into his courts. PSALM 96:8

Prayer: O glorious Jesus, in whom we live and without whom we die; quicken our hearts with thy holy love, that we may no longer esteem the vanities of the world, but place our affections entirely on thee, who didst die for our sins and rise again for our justification. Amen. JOHN WESLEY

Sentence: ...let us not love in word, neither in tongue; but in deed and in truth. And hereby we know that we are of the truth, and shall assure our hearts before him.

I JOHN 3:18-19

Prayer: Now to that God, who has suffered so much for us, who at one giving has conferred on us so many good things, and will yet confer so many more, to this God let every creature who is in heaven or upon the earth, in the sea or in the depth of the abyss, render praise, glory, honour and blessing. Amen.

FRANCIS OF ASSISI

Sentence: And Abel, he also brought of the firstlings of his flock and of the fat thereof. And the Lord had respect unto Abel and to his offering: But unto Cain and to his offering he had not respect....

GENESIS 4:4

Prayer: O glorious and almighty God, in whom all the spirits of the blessed, place the confidence of their hope; grant to us that, by Thy help, we may be able ever to serve Thee with a pure mind, and able to give of our means to Thy Kingdom with holy motives; through Jesus Christ our Lord. Amen.

SARUM BREVIARY (adapted)

Sentence: Take heed that ye do not your alms before men, to be seen of them: otherwise ye have no reward of your Father which is in heaven.

MATTHEW 6:1

Prayer: O God, let us seek true greatness. Show us that it is found only by humbling ourselves. Thou dost confound the proud who foster envy, criticism, and slander. But to the humble, who are hidden and content to be forgotten, thou dost reward in this life and in the next. Give us the capacity to give of ourselves and of our means in this humble spirit of Christ. Amen.

FRANÇOIS FÉNELON (adapted)

37

Sentence: ...Remember the words of the Lord Jesus, how he said, It is more blessed to give than to receive. Acts 20:35

Prayer: O God... the true Light of faithful souls and perfect Brightness of the Blessed, Who art verily the Light of the world, grant that our hearts may both render Thee a worthy prayer, and always glorify Thee with the offering of praises; through Jesus Christ our Lord. Amen.

GELASIAN SACRAMENTARY

Sentence: But seek ye first the kingdom of God, and his righteousness; and all these things shall be added unto you.

MATTHEW 6:33

Prayer: Surely, O God, Thy kingdom is not for those who do not love Thee. And if we love Thee, we cannot be indifferent to Thy kindness, inspiration, and grace. In gratitude we give thee what we have and what we are. Amen.

FRANÇOIS FÉNELON (adapted)

Sentence: For what shall it profit a man, if he shall gain the whole world, and lose his own soul? MARK 8:36

Prayer: Lord, our God, we give to Thee all we have and are, and vehemently desire, if we might know how, to do more for Thy love. Amen. FRANCIS OF ASSISI (adapted)

Sentence: And he that taketh not his cross and followeth after me, is not worthy of me. He that findeth his life shall lose it: and he that loseth his life for my sake shall find it.

MATTHEW 10:38-39

Prayer: Govern by Thy will the works of our hands; and lead us in the right way, that we may do what is well-pleasing and acceptable to Thee, that through us unworthy Thy holy name may be glorified. Amen. ST. BASIL

Sentence: Bring ye all the tithes into the storehouse, that there may be meat in mine house, and prove me now herewith, saith the Lord of hosts, if I will not open you the windows of heaven, and pour you out a blessing, that there shall not be room enough to receive it.   MALACHI 3:10

Prayer: Almighty God, who hast made all things for man, and man for Thy glory, sanctify our body and soul, our thoughts and our intentions, our words and actions, our gifts and giving, that whatsoever we shall think, or speak, or do or give, may by us be designed to the glorification of Thy name, and by Thy blessing, it may be effectual and successful in the work of God. Amen.   THOMAS À KEMPIS (adapted)

Sentence: ...If any man will come after me, let him deny himself, and take up his cross, and follow me.

MATTHEW 16:24

Prayer: O Lord our God, teach us, we beseech Thee, to ask Thee aright for the right blessings. Renew a willing spirit within us. Let Thy Spirit curb our wayward senses, and guide and enable us unto that which is our true good, to keep Thy laws, and in all our works evermore to rejoice in Thy glorious and gladdening Presence. For Thine is the glory and praise ...forever and ever. Amen.   ST. BASIL

Sentence: ...The children of Israel may bring their sacrifices ...unto the Lord, unto the door of the tabernacle of the congregation, unto the priest, and offer them for peace-offerings unto the Lord.   LEVITICUS 17:5

Prayer: Receive, O Lord, my entire liberty — my understanding, my memory, my will. From thee I have received all things; to thee do I return all things. Give me but thy grace and thy love. I ask not anything else of thee. Amen.

IGNATIUS LOYOLA

Sentence: And whosoever shall give to drink unto one of these little ones a cup of cold water only in the name of a disciple, verily I say unto you, he shall in no wise lose his reward.   MATTHEW 10:42

Prayer: O Thou Good Omnipotent, Who so carest for every one of us, as if Thou caredst for him alone; and so for all, as if all were but one! To Thee will I intrust whatsoever I have received from Thee, so shall I lose nothing. Amen.

ST. AUGUSTINE

Sentence: Every man according as he purposeth in his heart, so let him give; not grudgingly, or of necessity: for God loveth a cheerful giver.   II CORINTHIANS 9:7

Prayer: Almighty God, preserve us from all spiritual pride and the vainglory of temporal fame or name. Help us to call upon thy holy name in all our needs and wants. Grant that we in all our means, words and works may honor and praise thee alone. Amen.   MARTIN LUTHER

Sentence: For ye know the grace of our Lord Jesus Christ, that, though he was rich, yet for your sakes he became poor, that ye through his poverty might be rich.

II CORINTHIANS 8:9

Prayer: Take thou the full possession of my heart, raise there thy throne, and command there as thou dost in heaven. Being created by thee, let me live to thee. Being created for thee, let me ever act for thy glory. Being redeemed by thee, let me render unto thee what is thine, and let my spirit ever cleave to thee alone. Amen.   JOHN WESLEY

Offertory Sentences and Prayers for Holy Days

THE NEW YEAR

Sentence: Moreover his mother made him a little coat, and brought it to him from year to year, when she came up with her husband to offer the yearly sacrifice.   I SAMUEL 2:19

Prayer: We thank thee, heavenly Father, through Jesus Christ thy beloved Son, that thou hast preserved us this past year from all danger and harm; and we beseech thee to safeguard us in the new year from sin and all evil, that in all our thoughts and life we may please thee. We commit our bodies and souls and all we have into thy hand. Amen.

MARTIN LUTHER (adapted)

PALM SUNDAY

Sentence: Thou art my God, and I will praise thee: thou art my God, I will exalt thee. O give thanks unto the Lord; for he is good: for his mercy endureth for ever.

PSALM 118:28-29

Prayer: Lord Jesus Christ! Thou Light of Glory and image of the heavenly Father, as Thou art the true Light which illuminates all men, enlighten us so that we may be freed from our blindness of heart and be enabled to follow Thee with true faith, holy living and holy giving; so that our fellowship may be with the honored and exalted Christ, and the Father, and the Holy Spirit. Amen.   JOHANN ARNDT (adapted)

GOOD FRIDAY

Sentence: ...Worthy is the Lamb that was slain to receive power, and riches, and wisdom, and strength, and honor, and glory, and blessing.   REVELATION 5:12

41

Prayer: Almighty and everlasting God, by whose Spirit the whole body of the Church is governed and sanctified; Receive our gifts which we offer before thee for thy Holy Church; through our Lord and Saviour who gave so much for us.

THE BOOK OF COMMON PRAYER (adapted)

EASTER

Sentence: ...Thanks be to God, which giveth us the victory through our Lord Jesus Christ. Therefore, my beloved brethren, be ye steadfast, unmoveable, always abounding in the work of the Lord, forasmuch as ye know that your labor is not in vain in the Lord. I CORINTHIANS 15:57-58

Prayer: Blest be our everlasting Lord,
        Our Father, God, and King;
    Thy sovereign greatness we record,
        Thy glorious power we sing.
    By Thee the victory is given,
        The majesty divine;
    And strength, and might, and earth and heaven
        And all therein is Thine. Amen.

CHARLES WESLEY

ASCENSION SUNDAY

Sentence: For it is God which worketh in you both to will and to do of his good pleasure. PHILIPPIANS 2:13

Prayer: Come let us rise with Christ our Head
        And seek the things above,
    By the almighty Spirit led
        And filled with faith and love;
    Our hearts detached from all below
        Should after Him ascend,
    And only wish the joy to know
        Of our triumphant Friend.

CHARLES WESLEY

PENTECOST SUNDAY (WHITSUNDAY)

Sentence: If ye then, being evil, know how to give good gifts unto your children: how much more shall your heavenly Father give the Holy Spirit to them that ask him?

LUKE 11:13

Prayer: Come, O Holy Spirit, replenish the hearts of thy faithful believers, and kindle in them the fire of thy love.... O take all dissension and discord out of thy holy church and make us to be of one mind and of one loving giving heart. Amen. COVERDALE (adapted)

CHRISTMAS

Sentence: Vow, and pay unto the Lord your God: let all that be round about him bring presents unto him that ought to be feared. PSALM 76:11

Prayer: We give thanks to thee, almighty God, for revealing thyself to us, for sending thy Son Jesus Christ, that he might become a sacrifice, that through him we might be forgiven and receive eternal life. We give thanks to thee, O God, for making us a recipient of thy great favor through the gospel... and for preserving thy Word and thy holy church. O that we might truly declare thy goodness and blessings! Inflame us, we earnestly beseech thee, with thy Holy Spirit, that thanksgiving may shine forth in our lives. Amen. MELANCHTHON

Offertory Sentences and Prayers for Special Sundays

RACE RELATIONS SUNDAY (BROTHERHOOD DAY)

Sentence: Honor all men. Love the brotherhood. Fear God.... I PETER 2:17

Prayer: To thee, O Son of God, Lord Jesus Christ, as thou prayest to the eternal Father, we pray, make us one in him. Accept these our gifts, and may they contribute to lightening the distress of our society. Receive us into the fellowship of those who believe. Turn our hearts, O Christ, to everlasting truth and healing harmony. Amen. MELANCHTHON (adapted)

STEWARDSHIP SUNDAY (TITHING SUNDAY)

Sentence: Thou shalt truly tithe all the increase of thy seed, that the field bringeth forth year by year. DEUTERONOMY 14:22

Prayer: O Lord God Almighty, who didst endue Thy holy apostle Barnabas with singular gifts of the Holy Ghost; leave us not, we beseech Thee, destitute of Thy manifold gifts, nor yet of grace to use them always to Thy honour and glory; through Jesus Christ our Lord. Amen. EPISTLE OF BARNABAS

CHRISTIAN EDUCATION SUNDAY

Sentence: Buy the truth, and sell it not; also wisdom and instruction and understanding. PROVERBS 23:23

Prayer: O God, thou that of thy grace and fatherly love hast given such good and excellent gifts with singular light in all sciences; grant unto such as be learned a heart and mind that in all things they may have respect only to thy glory, and that in all their readings, writings, teachings, and doctrines they may prefer the same. Grant that our studies be not heathenish but godly and Christian; and accept these our gifts for the ongoing of truly Christian learning. Amen.

COVERDALE (adapted)

MOTHER'S DAY (FAMILY SUNDAY)

Sentence: Who can find a virtuous woman? for her price is far above rubies. She stretcheth out her hand to the poor; yea, she reacheth forth her hands to the needy.

PROVERBS 31:10, 20

Prayer: O Lord, give us, we beseech Thee, in the name of Jesus Christ Thy Son our God, that love which characterizes our mothers; that love which can never cease, that outgoing, giving love that will kindle our lamps but not extinguish them, that they may burn in us and enlighten others. Amen.

COLUMBA (adapted)

MEMORIAL SUNDAY

Sentence: For whosoever will save his life shall lose it; but whosoever shall lose his life for my sake and the gospel's, the same shall save it.   MARK 8:35

Prayer: O Lord Jesus Christ, who art the ineffable joy of Christians... make us Thine in all things. We beseech Thee to hear us, O Lord. Amen.   MOZARABIC BREVIARY

LABOR DAY SUNDAY

Sentence: For we are laborers together with God....

I CORINTHIANS 3:9

Prayer: Almighty God, our heavenly Father, who declarest thy glory and showest forth thy handiwork in the heavens and in the earth; Deliver us, we beseech thee, in our several callings, from the service of mammon, that we may do the work which thou givest us to do, in truth, in beauty, and in right-eousness, with singleness of heart as thy servants, and to the benefit of our fellow men; for the sake of him who came among us as one that serveth, thy Son Jesus Christ our Lord. Amen.

THE BOOK OF COMMON PRAYER

INDEPENDENCE SUNDAY

Sentence: ...What doth the Lord thy God require of thee, but to fear the Lord.... to walk in all his ways, and to love him, and to serve the Lord thy God with all thy heart and with all thy soul, To keep the commandments of the Lord, and his statutes, which I command thee this day for thy good?

DEUTERONOMY 10:12-13

Prayer: Almighty God, our heavenly Father, guide, we beseech thee, our Nation into the way of justice and truth, mercy and love, giving and forgiving; and establish among us that peace which is the fruit of righteousness, that we may become partakers of the Kingdom of our Lord and Saviour Jesus Christ. Amen.   THE BOOK OF COMMON PRAYER (adapted)

WORLD WIDE COMMUNION SUNDAY

Sentence: Yes in this ordinance divine
We still the sacred load may bear;
And now we in Thy offering join,
Thy sacramental passion share.

CHARLES WESLEY

Prayer: Lord Jesus! Thine is the glory! Plant true humility in our hearts! Grant us simplicity of spirit! Teach us to learn through humility how to gain true peace and unity! Teach us to follow Thy example of self-giving, O Jesus of the Cross! Amen.   JOHANN ARNDT (adapted)

MEN AND MISSIONS SUNDAY

Sentence: ...Come over into Macedonia, and help us.

ACTS 16:9

Prayer: Grant, almighty God, that we may join intelligence with zeal in building up thy church. As each of us is endowed with gifts, so may each strive for the edification of his brethren near and far, by giving what we have and are. Amen.

JOHN CALVIN (adapted)

46

REFORMATION SUNDAY

Sentence: I am crucified with Christ: nevertheless I live; yet not I, but Christ liveth in me: and the life which I now live in the flesh I live by the faith of the Son of God, who loved me, and gave himself for me.   GALATIANS 2:20

Prayer: Almighty and everlasting God, who by thy Holy Spirit dost govern and sanctify the whole Christian church: Hear our prayers... and grant that by thy grace we may serve thee in true faith; through Jesus Christ, thy Son, our Lord. Amen.   MARTIN LUTHER

WORLD PEACE SUNDAY (WORLD ORDER SUNDAY)

Sentence: Be not deceived; God is not mocked: for whatsoever a man soweth, that shall he also reap. And let us not be weary in well doing: for in due season we shall reap, if we faint not.   GALATIANS 6:7, 9

Prayer: O merciful Lord, who hast made of one Blood and redeemed by one Ransom all Nations of Men, let me never harden my heart against any that partake of the same Nature and Redemption with me, but grant me Universal Charity towards all Men. Give me, O Thou Father of Compassions, such a tenderness and meltingness of Heart that I may be deeply affected with all the Miseries and Calamities outward or inward of my Brethren, and diligently keep them in Love.
                    THOMAS À KEMPIS

THANKSGIVING SUNDAY

Sentence: Then the disciples, every man according to his ability, determined to send relief unto the brethren which dwelt in Judaea: Which also they did, and sent it to the elders by the hands of Barnabas and Saul.   ACTS 11:29-30

47

Prayer: Most gracious God ... We yield thee unfeigned thanks and praise for the return of seed-time and harvest, for the increase of the ground and the gathering in of the fruits thereof, and for all the other blessings of thy merciful providence bestowed upon this nation and people. And, we beseech thee, give us a just sense of these great mercies; such as may appear in our lives by an humble, holy, and obedient walking before thee all our days; through Jesus Christ our Lord.... Amen. THE BOOK OF COMMON PRAYER

UNIVERSAL BIBLE SUNDAY

Sentence: Blessed are they that keep his testimonies, and that seek him with the whole heart. PSALM 119:2

Prayer: Make me to go in the path of thy commandments; for therein do I delight. Incline my heart unto thy testimonies, and not to coveteousness. Amen. PSALM 119:35-36

LAYMEN'S DAY

Sentence: Remember all thy offerings, and accept thy burnt-sacrifice. PSALM 20:3

Prayer: O Lord God! All that I am and all that I have is Thy gift. Thou hast given me this not for my own good but that I might thereby seek Thy honour and glory, sharing it for Thy praise and my neighbor's good. O! let me ever be a true steward of Thy gifts so that Thou mayest say: Well done, Thou good and faithful servant. Amen. JOHANN ARNDT

IV. BENEDICTIONS

BENEDICTIONS

The Lord bless thee, and keep thee: The Lord make his face shine upon thee, and be gracious unto thee: The Lord lift up his countenance upon thee, and give thee peace. Amen.

NUMBERS 6:24-26

To the Holy Spirit that sanctifies us, with the Father that made and created us, and the Son that redeemed us, be given all honor and glory, world without end. Amen.

THOMAS CRANMER

The grace of the Lord Jesus Christ, and the love of God, and the communion of the Holy Ghost, be with you all. Amen.

II CORINTHIANS 13:14

God be merciful unto us, and bless us; and cause his face to shine upon us. Amen.

PSALMS 67:1

Farewell in God our Father and in Jesus Christ, our common hope. Amen.

IGNATIUS LOYOLA

The grace of our Lord Jesus Christ be with you and with all, in every place, who have been called by God through him, through whom be to him glory, honour, power and greatness and eternal dominion, from eternity to eternity. Amen.

I CLEMENT

Brethren, the grace of our Lord Jesus Christ be with your spirit. Amen.

GALATIANS 6:18

The Lord of glory and of all grace be with your spirit. Amen.

EPISTLE OF BARNABAS

Peace be to the brethren, and love with faith, from God the Father and the Lord Jesus Christ. Grace be with all them that love our Lord Jesus Christ in sincerity. Amen.

EPHESIANS 6:23-24

The great Bishop of our souls, Jesus our Lord, so strengthen and assist your troubled hearts with the mighty comfort of the Holy Spirit, that neither earthly tyrants, nor worldly torments, may have power to drive you from the hope and expectation of that kingdom, which for the elect was prepared from the beginning, by our heavenly Father, to whom be all praise and honor, now and ever. Amen.   JOHN KNOX

The almighty God, Father of our Lord and Savior, Jesus Christ, mercifully protect you, strengthen you, and guide you. Amen.   MELANCHTHON

The grace of our Lord Jesus Christ be with you all. Amen.

REVELATION 22:21

May our dear Lord Jesus Christ show you his hands and his side, and with his love put joy into your hearts, and may you behold and hear only him until you find your joy in him. Amen.   MARTIN LUTHER

The mighty God of Jacob be with you to supplant his enemies, and give you the favor of Joseph; and the wisdom and the spirit of Stephen be with your heart and with your mouth, and teach your lips what they shall say, and how to answer all things. He is our God, if we despair in ourselves, and trust in him; and his is the glory. Amen.

WILLIAM TYNDALE

God, the Father of our Lord Jesus Christ, who is the Father of glory, and God of all consolation, give you the Spirit of wisdom, and open unto you the knowledge of himself by means of his dear Son. Amen.   JOHN KNOX

Grace and peace from God Almighty be multiplied to you
through Jesus Christ. Amen.   I CLEMENT

I am Alpha and Omega, the beginning and the end, the first
and the last. Blessed are they that do his commandments, that
they may have right to the tree of life, and may enter in
through the gates into the city. Amen.
REVELATION 22:13-14

The grace of God the Father and the peace of our Lord Jesus
Christ, through the fellowship of the Holy Spirit, dwell with
us forever. Amen.   JOHN CALVIN

...Peace be with you all that are in Christ Jesus. Amen.
I PETER 5:14

...The Lord watch between me and thee, when we are absent
one from another. Amen.   GENESIS 31:49

Benedictions for Holy Days

THE NEW YEAR

Now unto him that is able to keep you from falling, and to present you faultless before the presence of his glory with exceeding joy, To the only wise God our Saviour, be glory and majesty, dominion and power, both now and ever. Amen.

JUDE 24-25

PALM SUNDAY

To him be glory and dominion for ever and ever. Amen.

I PETER 5:11

GOOD FRIDAY

Now the God of Peace, that brought again from the dead our Lord Jesus, that great shepherd of the sheep, through the blood of the everlasting covenant, Make you perfect in every good work to do his will, working in you that which is well-pleasing in his sight, through Jesus Christ; to whom be glory for ever and ever. Amen.   HEBREWS 13:20-21

EASTER

Now may God and the Father of our Lord Jesus Christ, and the 'eternal priest' himself, Jesus Christ, the Son of God, build you up in the faith and truth, and in all gentleness, and without wrath, and in patience, and in longsuffering, and endurance, and purity, and may he give you lot and part with his saints, and to us with you, and to all under heaven who shall believe in our Lord and God Jesus Christ and in his 'Father who raised him from the dead.' Amen.   POLYCARP

ASCENSION SUNDAY

> The Lord of Hosts is He,
>   The omnipotent I AM,
> Glorious in majesty,
>   Jehovah is His name.

Wide open throw the heavenly scene;
Receive the King of glory in.

CHARLES WESLEY

PENTECOST SUNDAY (WHITSUNDAY)

Now unto him that is able to do exceeding abundantly above all that we ask or think, according to the power that worketh in us, Unto him be glory in the church by Christ Jesus throughout all ages, world without end. Amen.

EPHESIANS 3:20-21

CHRISTMAS

To the only wise God our Saviour, be glory and majesty, dominion and power, both now and ever. Amen.

JUDE 25

RACE RELATIONS SUNDAY (BROTHERHOOD DAY)

Now may the blessing of the Father of our Lord Jesus Christ, of whom the whole family in heaven and earth is named, grant you, according to the riches of his glory, to be strengthened with might by his Spirit in the inner man; that Christ may dwell in your hearts by faith and be filled with the fulness of God. Amen.   EPHESIANS 3:14-19 (adapted)

STEWARDSHIP SUNDAY (TITHING SUNDAY)

May God, who seeth all things, and who is the Ruler of all spirits and the Lord of all flesh — who chose our Lord Jesus Christ and us through Him to be a peculiar people — grant to every soul that calleth upon His glorious and holy Name, faith, peace, patience, long-suffering, self-control, purity, and sobriety, to the well-pleasing of His Name, through our High Priest and Guardian Jesus Christ; to whom be glory and majesty, might and honour, both now and to all eternity. Amen.   I CLEMENT (slightly adapted)

CHRISTIAN EDUCATION SUNDAY

May the God of our Lord Jesus Christ, the Father of glory, give you the spirit of wisdom and revelation in the knowledge of Him.   EPHESIANS 1:17 (adapted)

MOTHER'S DAY (FAMILY SUNDAY)

Now may the blessing of God, the Father of our Lord Jesus Christ, of whom the whole family in heaven and earth is named, be with you and all God's children, this day and for-ever more. Amen.   EPHESIANS 3:14-15 (adapted)

MEMORIAL SUNDAY

But may the God of all grace, who hath called us unto his eternal glory by Christ Jesus, after that ye have suffered a while, make you perfect, stablish, strengthen, settle you. To him be glory and dominion for ever and ever. Amen.

I Peter 5:10-11

LABOR DAY SUNDAY

...Be ye steadfast, unmovable, always abounding in the work of the Lord, forasmuch as ye know that your labor is not in vain in the Lord. Amen.　　　　I Corinthians 15:58

INDEPENDENCE SUNDAY

Stand fast therefore in the liberty wherewith Christ hath made us free, and be not entangled again with the yoke of bondage. Amen.　　　　Galatians 5:1

WORLD WIDE COMMUNION SUNDAY

...Let the peace of God rule in your hearts, to the which also ye are called in one body; and be ye thankful. Amen.

Colossians 3:15

MEN AND MISSIONS SUNDAY

Now to him that is of power to stablish you according to my gospel, and the preaching of Jesus Christ, according to the revelation of the mystery, which was kept secret since the world began, But now is made manifest, and by the Scriptures of the prophets, according to the commandment of the everlasting God, made known to all nations for the obedience of faith: To God only wise, be glory through Jesus Christ for ever. Amen.　　　　Romans 16:25-27

REFORMATION SUNDAY

Grace be unto you, and peace, from God our Father, and from the Lord Jesus Christ. Amen.　　　　I Corinthians 1:3

WORLD PEACE SUNDAY (WORLD ORDER SUNDAY)

...Be perfect, be of good comfort, be of one mind, live in peace; and the God of love and peace shall be with you. Amen.   II Corinthians 13:11

THANKSGIVING SUNDAY

...Thanks be to God, which giveth us the victory through our Lord Jesus Christ. Amen.   I Corinthians 15:57

UNIVERSAL BIBLE SUNDAY

Let the word of Christ dwell in you richly in all wisdom.... Amen.   Colossians 3:16

LAYMEN'S DAY

...Grow in grace, and in the knowledge of our Lord and Saviour Jesus Christ. To him be glory both now and for ever. Amen.   II Peter 3:18

INDEXES

Index of Scripture Verses

Index of Persons, Holy Days, Special Sundays, Etc.